XTREME WRESTLING ROYALTY

ROMAN REIGNS

A&D Xtreme
BOLD HI-LO NONFICTION
An imprint of Abdo Publishing
abdobooks.com

ALEX MONNIG

TAKE IT TO THE XTREME!

GET READY FOR AN EXTREME ADVENTURE! THE PAGES OF THIS BOOK WILL TAKE YOU INTO THE THRILLING WORLD OF PROFESSIONAL WRESTLING. WHEN YOU HAVE FINISHED READING THIS BOOK, TAKE THE XTREME CHALLENGE ON PAGE 45 ABOUT WHAT YOU'VE LEARNED!

ABDOBOOKS.COM
Published by Abdo Publishing, a division of ABDO, PO Box 398166, Minneapolis, Minnesota 55439.
Printed in the United States of America, North Mankato, MN.
052023
092023

THIS BOOK CONTAINS RECYCLED MATERIALS

Design: Kelly Doudna, Mighty Media, Inc.
Production: Mighty Media, Inc.
Editor: Katherine Chu
Cover Photograph: Arthur Cauty/Shutterstock Images
Interior Photographs: Alyssa Pointer/AP Images, pp. 8-9; Art Wager/iStockphoto, pp. 6-7; Arthur Cauty/Shutterstock Images, p. 44; Don Feria/AP Images, pp. 4-5, 34-35; Journalist 1st Class Kristin Fitzsimmons/Wikimedia Commons, p. 7; Karl Newton/SPP (Sport Press Photo)/AP Images, pp. 26-27; Manish Swarup/AP Images, pp. 36-37; Mark Hawkins/Alamy Photo, pp. 40-41; Megan Elice Meadows/Flickr, pp. 10-11, 12-13, 14-15, 18-19, 22-23; Miguel Discart/Flickr, pp. 16-17, 20-21, 28-29, 32-33; MOHAMED HUSSAIN YOUNIS/iStockphoto, pp. 42-43; REUTERS/Alamy Photo, p. 42; Tristan Reynaud/SIPA/AP Images, pp. 38-39; WENN Rights Ltd/Alamy Photo, pp. 30-31; Willy Sanjuan/AP Images, pp. 24-25; Xavier Collin/Image Press Agency/AP Images, p. 1
Design Elements: amgun/Shutterstock Images (perspective); sanchesnet1/iStockphoto (spikes color, bolts); Wth/Shutterstock Images (stripes)

LIBRARY OF CONGRESS CONTROL NUMBER: 2022948843

PUBLISHER'S CATALOGING-IN-PUBLICATION DATA
Names: Monnig, Alex, author.
Title: Roman Reigns / by Alex Monnig
Description: Minneapolis, Minnesota : Abdo Publishing, 2024 | Series: Xtreme wrestling royalty | Includes online resources and index.
Identifiers: ISBN 9781098291488 (lib. bdg.) | ISBN 9781098277949 (ebook)
Subjects: LCSH: Anoa'i, Leati Joseph, 1985---Juvenile literature. | Wrestlers--Biography--Juvenile literature. | Actors--Biography--Juvenile literature. | World Wrestling Entertainment, Inc--Juvenile literature.
Classification: DDC 796.812092--dc23

TABLE OF CONTENTS

CHAPTER 1

A FIGHT BETWEEN CHAMPIONS

In April 2022, Leati Joseph "Roman Reigns" Anoa'i and Brock Lesnar performed **incredible stunts** at WrestleMania XXXVII. Lesnar put Reigns in a wrestling hold. Reigns broke the hold and stopped Lesnar's finishing move. Then he drove his shoulder into Lesnar. Reigns won the match!

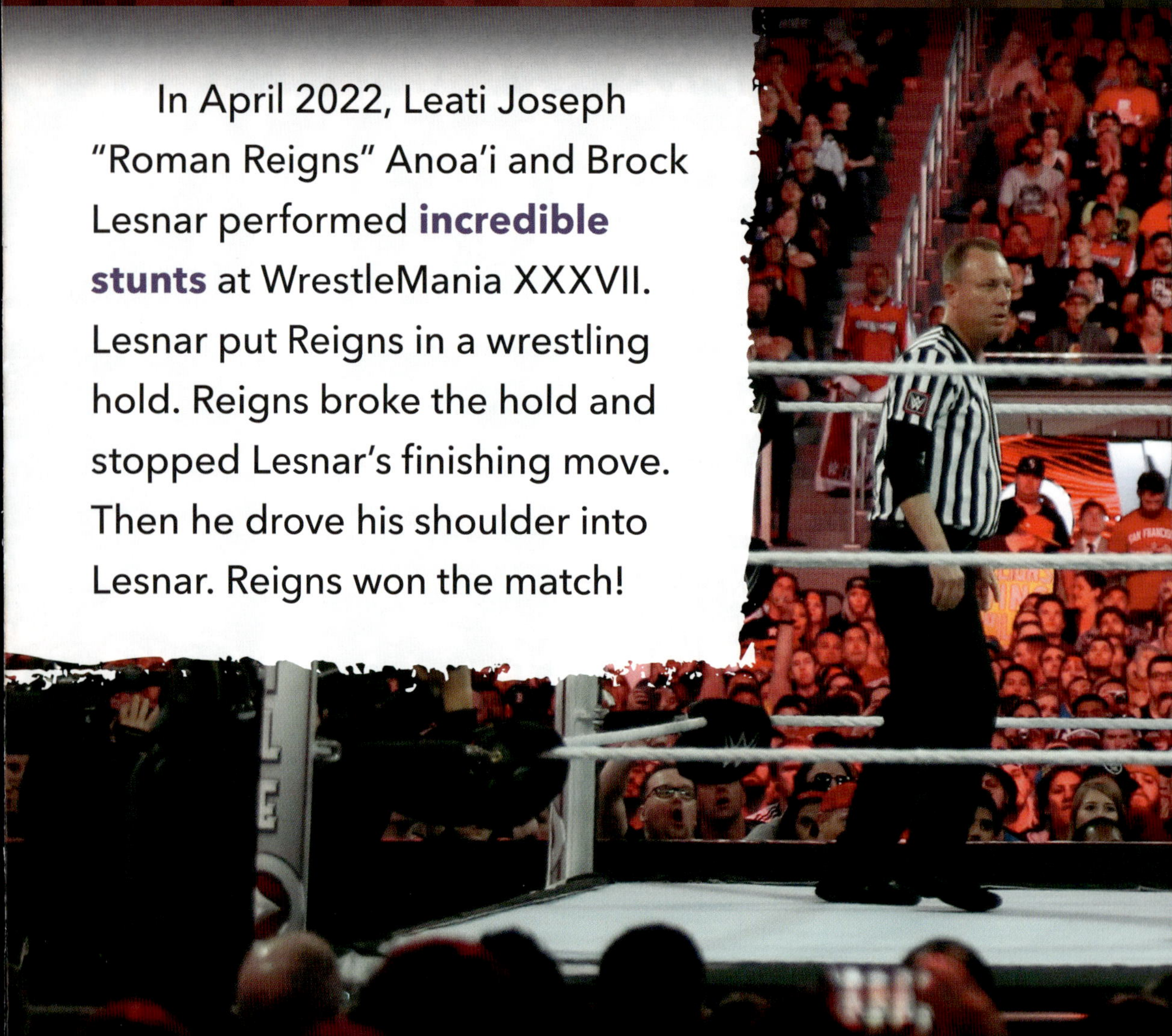

In 2015, Roman Reigns (*center*) fought Brock Lesnar (*right*) for the first time at WrestleMania XXXI.

CHAPTER 2

A FAMILY OF WRESTLERS

Leati Joseph Anoa'i was born on May 25, 1985, in Pensacola, Florida. His dad Sika Anoa'i wrestled for the World Wrestling Federation (WWF). In 2002, WWF would become World Wrestling Entertainment (WWE). It is a professional wrestling organization that features characters who perform in staged matches.

Leati grew up as part of a wrestling family in Pensacola. His older brother, Matthew "Rosey" Anoa'i (*pictured*) also wrestled for WWE from 2002 to 2006.

Reigns debuted Georgia Tech's new football uniform in 2018.

Leati had many dreams growing up. One was to join the National Football League (NFL). He played football in high school and college. Anoa'i attended the Georgia **Institute** of **Technology** (Georgia Tech). There, he was a **defensive lineman** and a team captain his **senior** year. He tried out for the NFL after finishing college in 2007. He didn't get picked. But Anoa'i had a backup plan.

XTREME FACT

Roman Reigns is related to famous wrestler Dwayne "the Rock" Johnson!

CHAPTER 3

ENTERING THE RING

Anoa'i knew if he didn't play football, he could wrestle for WWE. He had many family members who wrestled professionally. In 2010, WWE offered him a **developmental** contract. This meant Anoa'i would train at a smaller wrestling program. If he was good enough, Anoa'i could wrestle for WWE.

In 2014, Reigns fought hard but was defeated by Miroslav "Rusev" Barnyashev at a September SmackDown event.

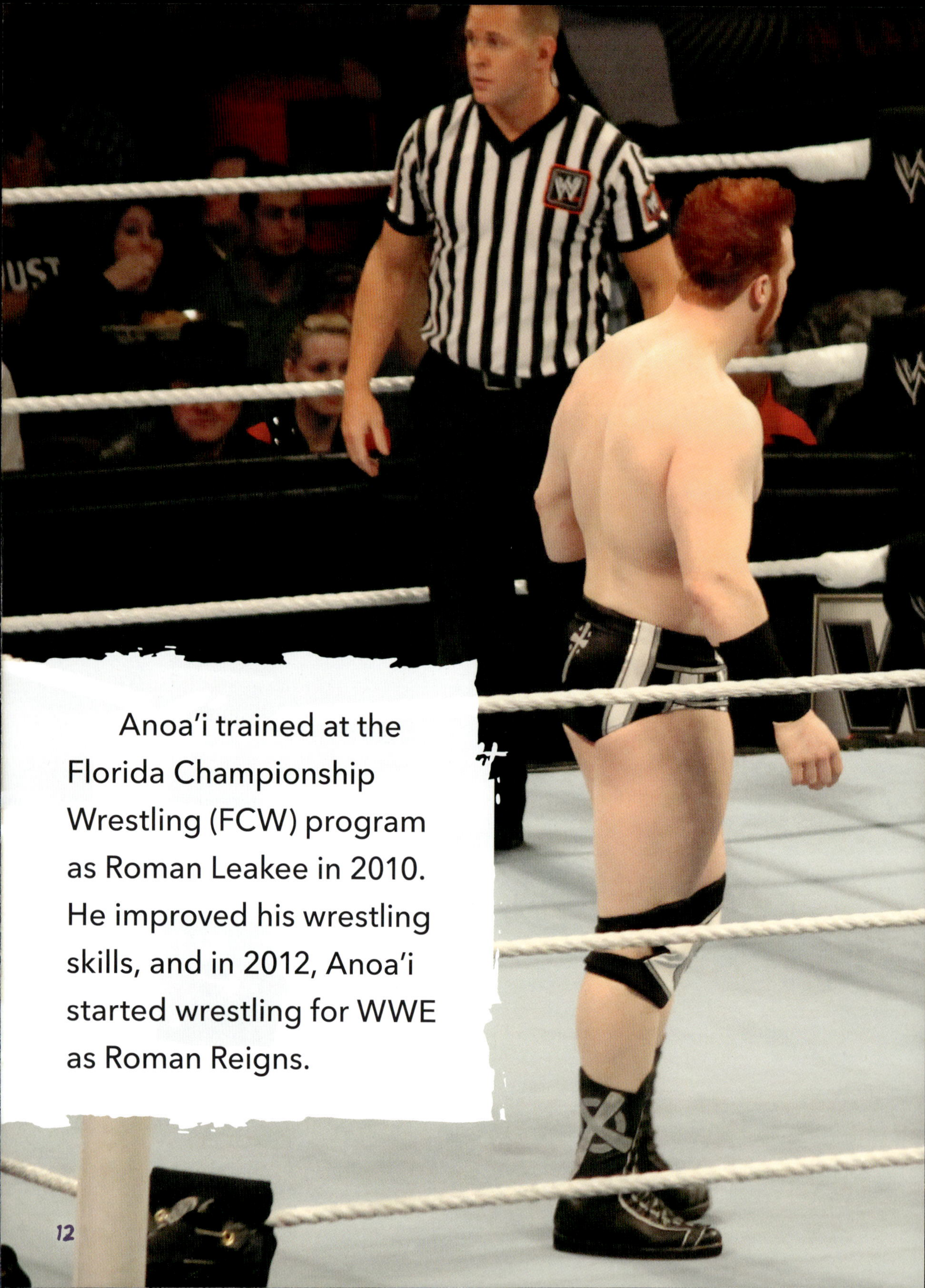

Anoa'i trained at the Florida Championship Wrestling (FCW) program as Roman Leakee in 2010. He improved his wrestling skills, and in 2012, Anoa'i started wrestling for WWE as Roman Reigns.

Reigns faces Stephen "Sheamus" Farrelly at WWE Raw in 2013. Reigns wanted to wrestle as just "Roman." WWE wanted him to have a last name, so he became Roman Reigns.

Reigns made his WWE **debut** at the 2012 Survivor Series event in November. His partners were Jonathan "Dean Ambrose" Good and Colby "Seth Rollins" Lopez. The three wrestlers were a tag team called the Shield. They stormed into the ring at the main event match. They slammed wrestler Ryan "Ryback" Reeves through a prop table, stunning the crowd.

XTREME FACT

Reigns isn't the only WWE wrestler to come from the FCW program. Ambrose, Rollins, Andrew "Drew McIntyre" Galloway, and Stephen "Sheamus" Farrelly all wrestled at FCW.

Reigns fought Rollins (*bottom*) during WWE Raw in 2014. Reigns, Rollins, and Ambrose worked well together at FCW, which led to them becoming the Shield team.

CHAPTER 4

THE SHIELD

The Shield team members were also known as "heels," or bad guys. They named themselves the Hounds of Justice. Reigns was called the Big Dog because many thought he was the **toughest** Shield member.

When Reigns (*center*), Ambrose (*right*), and Rollins (*left*) formed the Shield, they originally helped Phillip "CM Punk" Brooks defeat his enemies.

The Shield faced many wrestlers in the 18 months following their **debut**. They often used their **Triple** Powerbomb move against other wrestlers. Reigns roared as Ambrose and Rollins picked up their opponent. Then the trio threw their opponent onto the mat or through a prop table.

XTREME FACT

The Rock, John Cena, Allen "AJ Styles" Jones, and Mark "the Undertaker" Calaway were all victims of the Shield's Triple Powerbomb move.

The Shield (*left*) face a team called the Authority (*right*) at WWE Raw in 2014. The Authority consisted of wrestlers Paul Levesque (*fourth from right*), Randy Orton (*third from right*), and Dave Bautista (*second from right*).

CHAPTER 5

FEUDS AND FANS

Many wrestling teams lost to the Shield. The Shield's **feud** with a two-wrestler team called the Usos shocked many fans. This is because the Usos were Reigns's cousins Joshua "Jey Uso" Fatu and Jonathan "Jimmy Uso" Fatu. From May 2013 to January 2014, the two teams fought many times. But in July 2021, Reigns and the Usos would become a team called the Bloodline.

Jimmy Uso (*left*) and Jey Uso (*right*) would perform a traditional Samoan war dance called the Siva Tau before every match they fought in.

Each member of the Shield had his own personality. Ambrose (*right*) was the group leader, Reigns (*center*) was the muscle, and Rollins (*left*) was the hothead.

In 2014, the Shield fought a three-wrestler team called the Wyatt Family. The two teams faced each other at a February **Elimination** Chamber event. The Shield lost the match. But they remained popular with fans.

CHAPTER 6

FAMILY LIFE

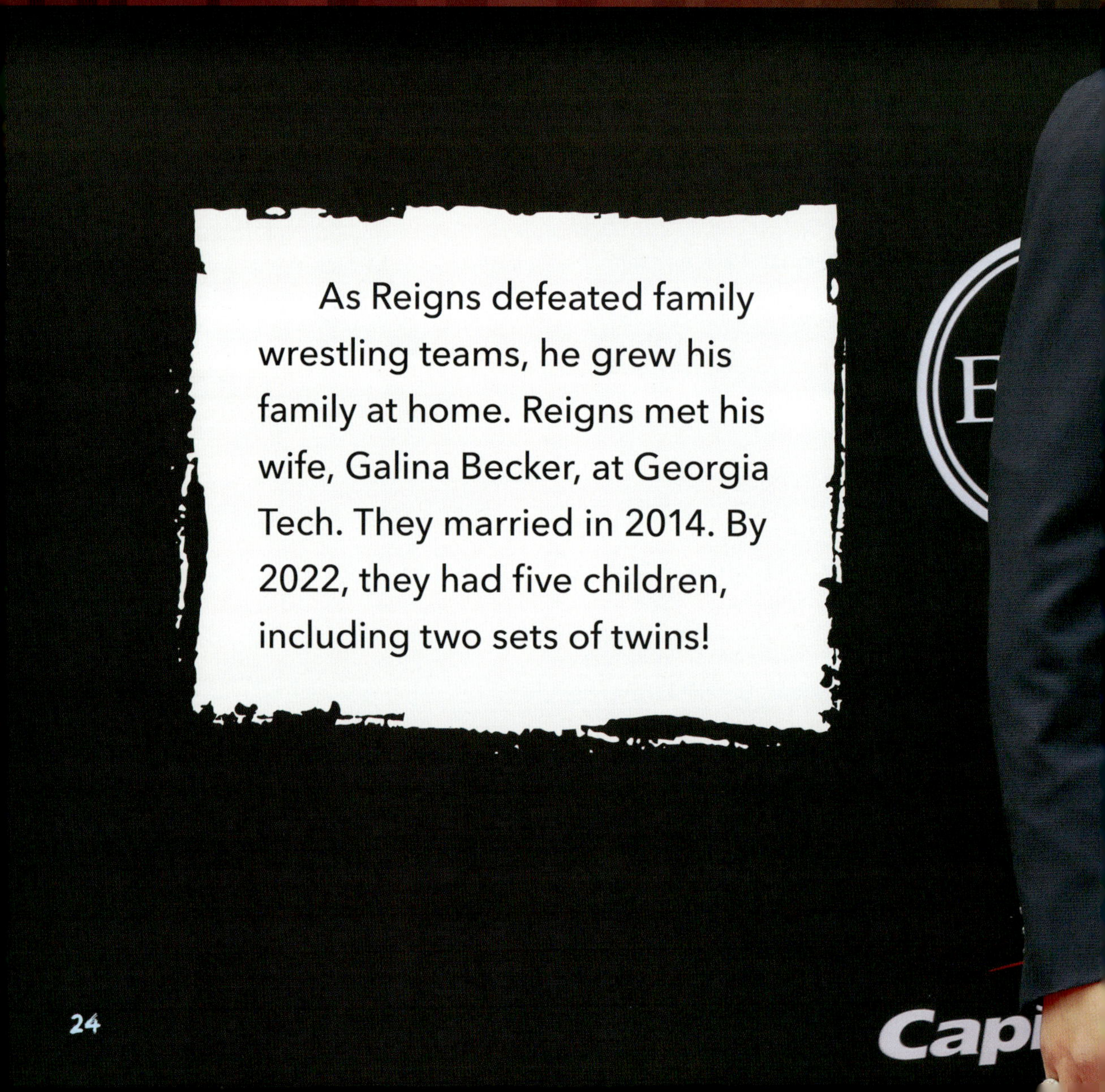

As Reigns defeated family wrestling teams, he grew his family at home. Reigns met his wife, Galina Becker, at Georgia Tech. They married in 2014. By 2022, they had five children, including two sets of twins!

Reigns with his daughter Joelle Reigns during the ESPY Awards in 2018

CHAPTER 7

FAMOUS MOVES

Reigns traded punches with McIntyre (*left*) at the WWE Clash at the Castle event in 2022. Reigns hit McIntyre with his famous spear move, winning the match.

The Shield members worked together like a family. But Reigns also had his own famous moves. Many fans loved his Superman Punch. Reigns would kick his leg forward. Then he would kick it back while throwing a punch, giving the punch more power. Reigns also used his spear move. He would run toward an opponent. Then he would jump and hit them with his shoulder.

CHAPTER 8

MAKING A NAME FOR HIMSELF

In 2014, Rollins attacked Ambrose and Reigns during a WWE Monday Night Raw event. This caused the Shield to break up. Reigns started wrestling on his own as a "face," or good guy. He even qualified to compete for the WWE Championship. Reigns wasn't successful, but he didn't give up.

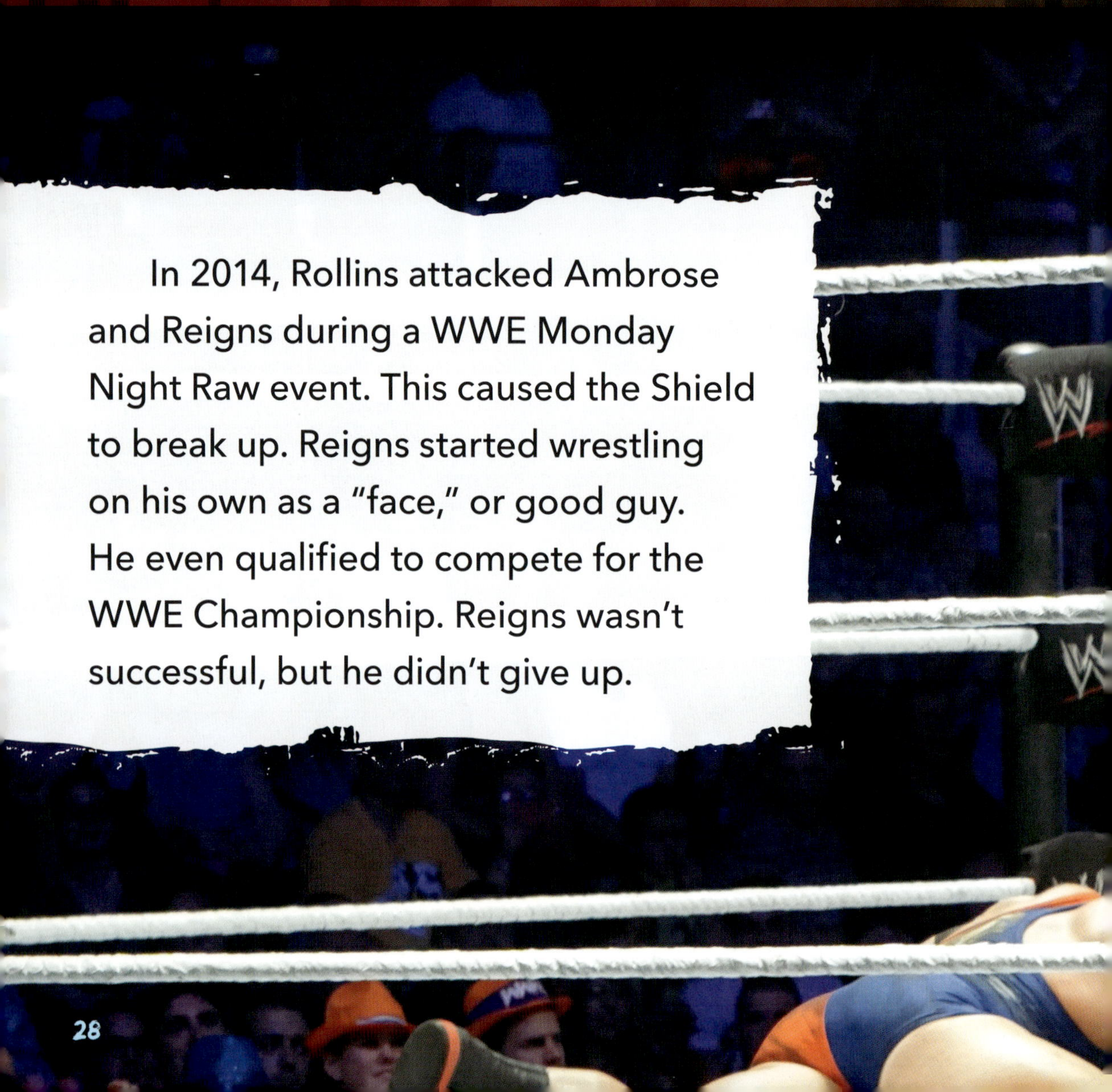

Reigns was so popular in 2014 that fans awarded him with the Slammy Award for Superstar of the Year.

Reigns holds up the WWE Tag Team Championship belt in 2013.

XTREME FACT

Reigns is a Grand Slam champion. This means he's won at least four different WWE championship title belts. Reigns won at least one Tag Team, Intercontinental, United States, WWE, and Universal Championship belt.

Reigns won the January Royal Rumble match in 2015. This gave him a spot to fight for the championship at the Survivor Series **tournament** in March. Reigns and Ambrose made it to the final match. Ambrose fought hard. But Reigns won with his spear move. Reigns was the WWE World Heavyweight Champion!

CHAPTER 9

TWO CHAMPIONSHIPS

Reigns and Lesnar's (*bottom*) feud lasted for eight years.

Reigns battled many wrestlers during his WWE career. But his biggest rival was Lesnar. Lesnar was one of the strongest wrestlers to ever enter the ring. Reigns and Lesnar's **feud** started in 2015.

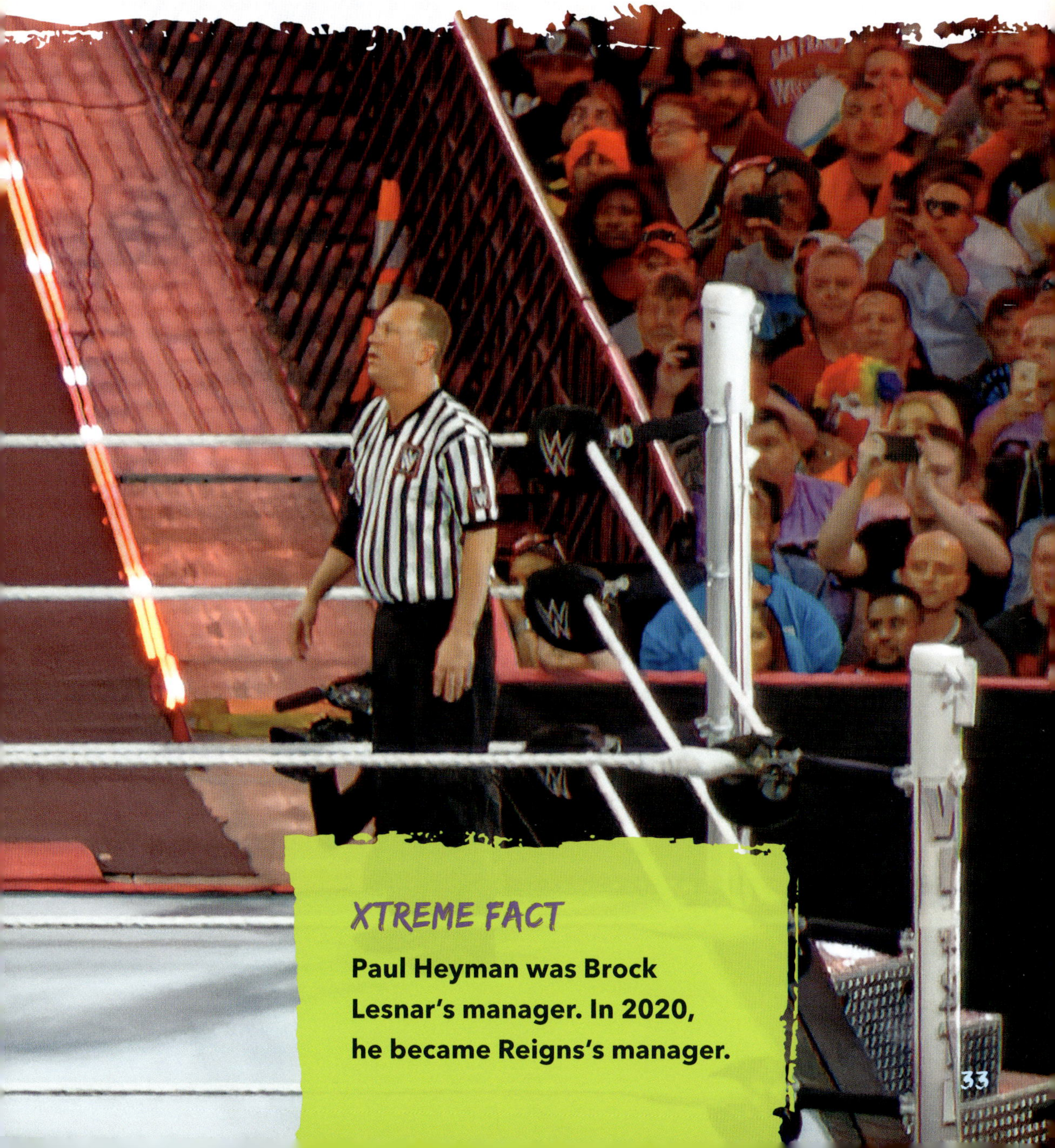

XTREME FACT

Paul Heyman was Brock Lesnar's manager. In 2020, he became Reigns's manager.

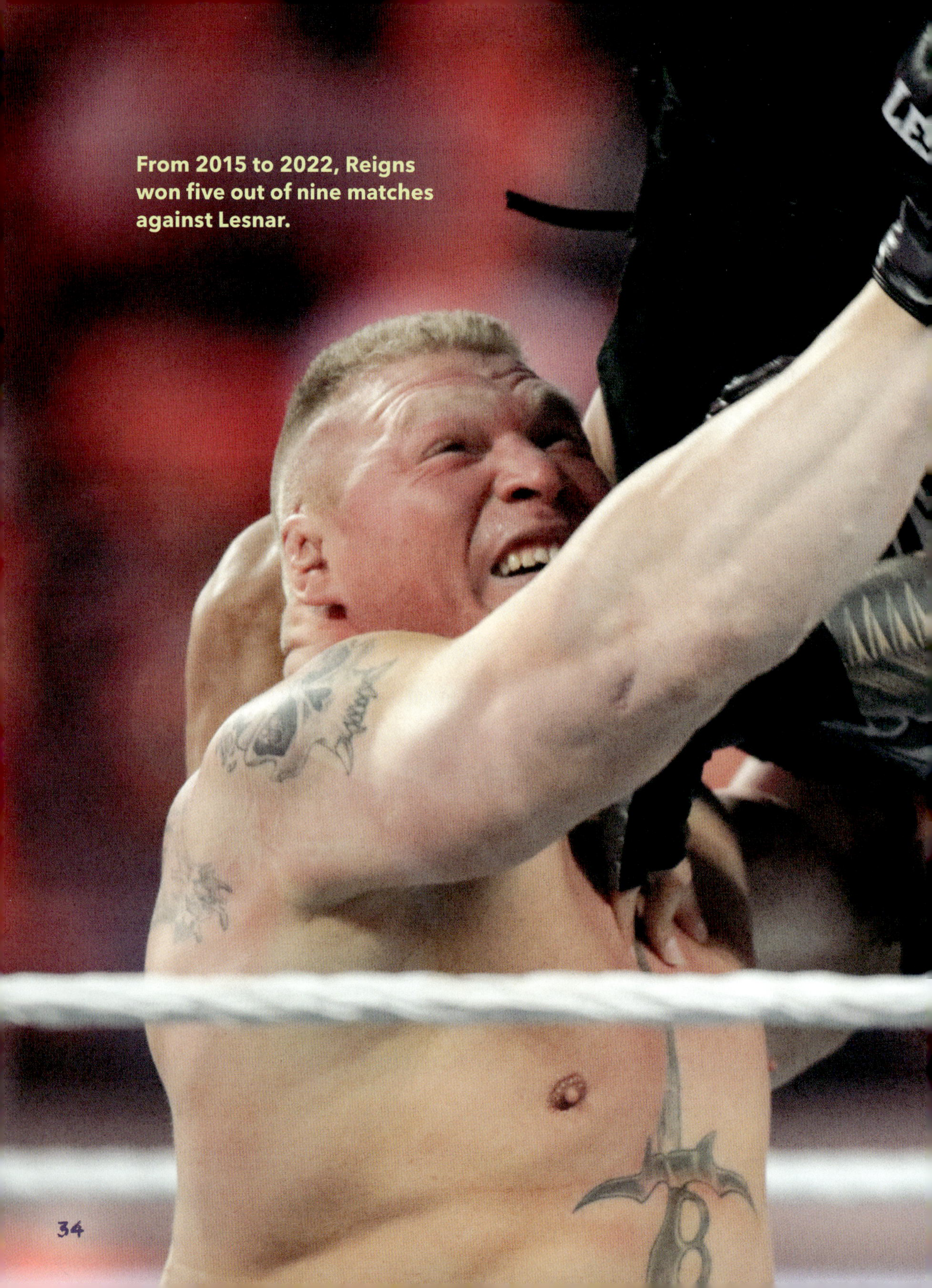

From 2015 to 2022, Reigns won five out of nine matches against Lesnar.

In March 2015, Reigns faced Lesnar at WrestleMania XXXI. WrestleMania is one of WWE's most important and popular annual events. Lesnar and Reigns fought hard. But Rollins interrupted the match. He defeated Reigns and Lesnar, winning the World Heavyweight Championship.

CHAPTER 10

OVERCOMING CHALLENGES

In 2016, Reigns hit the Big Show (*right*) with his Superman Punch three times, defeating him.

Reigns's popularity grew after WrestleMania XXXI in 2015. So did his **feuds**. He battled with Lesnar and Paul "the Big Show" Wight. Both wrestlers were huge and strong rivals. Reigns also fought with Windham "Bray Wyatt" Rotunda and Adam "Braun Strowman" Scherr.

Reigns celebrates his win at a WWE Live event in May 2018. On October 22, 2018, he announced that he had leukemia.

From December 2015 to October 2018, Reigns won two more WWE Championships and the Universal Championship. But in October he had to stop wrestling. He was sick with **leukemia**. Reigns received **treatment** to fight the **cancer**. His cancer went into **remission** in February 2019. Reigns was ready to wrestle once again.

XTREME FACT

Reigns first had leukemia in 2007. In 2019, he started working with the Leukemia & Lymphoma Society to raise awareness for children fighting cancer.

CHAPTER 11

THE REIGN OF REIGNS

Reigns fights McIntyre (*left*) in 2022. Between 2013 and 2022, the two fought each other in more than 100 matches.

The crowd cheered as Reigns returned to WWE at Monday Night Raw in February 2019. In the next 18 months, he won 107 out of 120 fights.

In August 2020, Reigns defeated Wyatt and Strowman, winning the Universal Championship.

Reigns defeated Lesnar (*bottom*) during the WWE Crown Jewel event in Riyadh, Saudi Arabia, in 2021.

After that win, Reigns **focused** on another goal. One of his favorite sayings is "I can, and I will." In April 2022, he defeated Lesnar at WrestleMania XXXVIII. Reigns became the first wrestler to hold both the WWE Championship and the Universal Championship!

XTREME FACT

Reigns held the Universal Championship for more than 900 days. He beat Lesnar's record of 503 days, which ended when Reigns defeated him in 2018.

CHAPTER 12

A TRUE WARRIOR

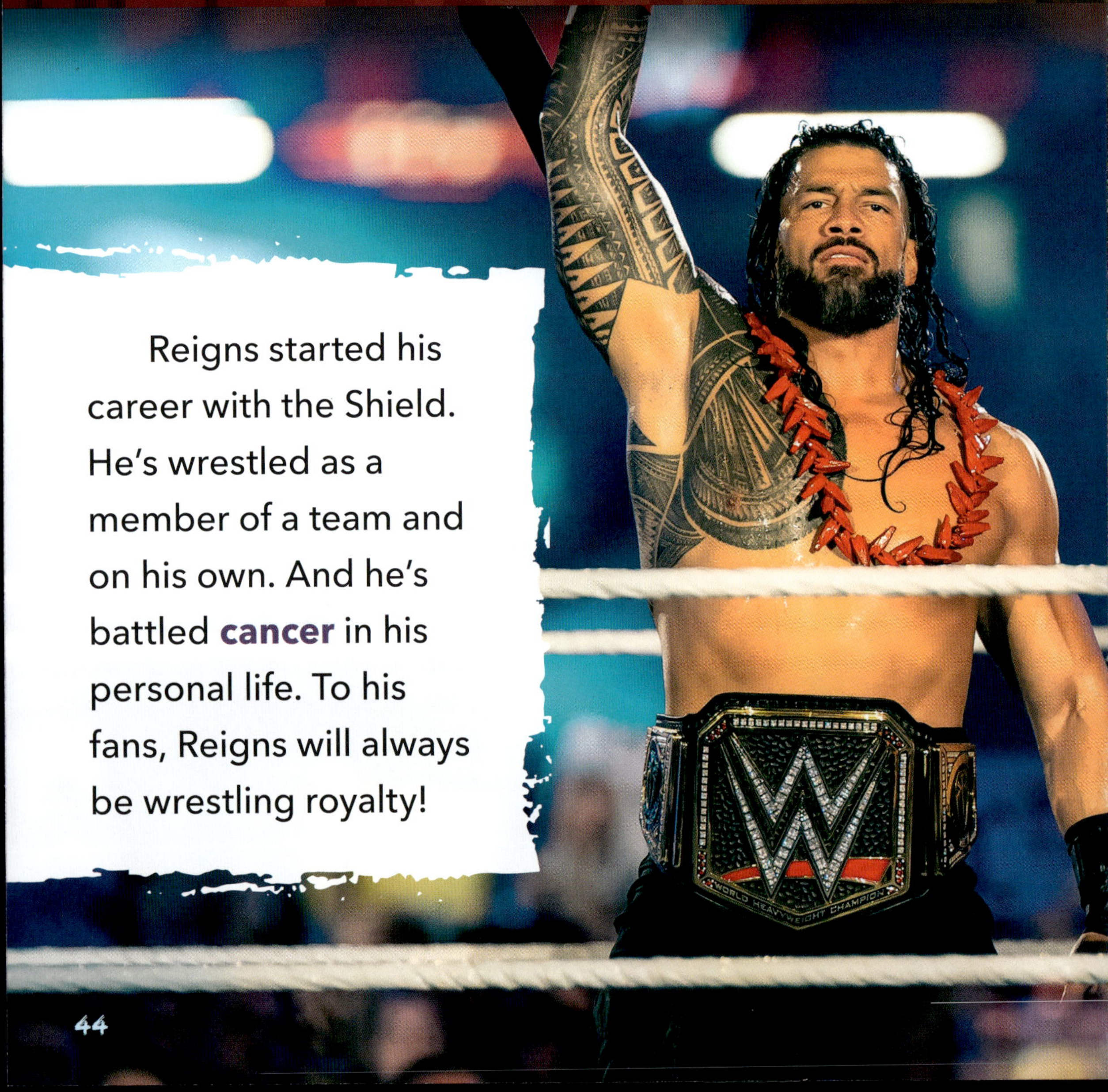

Reigns started his career with the Shield. He's wrestled as a member of a team and on his own. And he's battled **cancer** in his personal life. To his fans, Reigns will always be wrestling royalty!

XTREME CHALLENGE

TAKE THE QUIZ BELOW AND PUT WHAT YOU'VE LEARNED TO THE TEST!

1) What do you think it would feel like to hold a title for hundreds of days? Would you feel scared to lose it every time you wrestled? Or excited to defend your title?

2) What two title belts did Reigns hold in April 2022?

3) Would you rather be part of a tag team or wrestle on your own?

4) Who were the other two Shield members?

5) Where was Reigns sent to train after he signed his WWE developmental contract in 2010?

GLOSSARY

cancer–any of a group of very harmful diseases that cause a body's cells to become unhealthy.

debut–a first appearance.

defensive–related to keeping the other team from scoring in a game.

developmental–related to growing, changing, or improving over time.

elimination–the act or process of being removed from competition by being defeated.

feud–a long-lasting fight or disagreement.

focus–to concentrate on or pay particular attention to.

incredible–difficult to believe.

institute–an organization created for a certain purpose, such as research.

leukemia–a cancer where there is an abnormal increase in white blood cells in the tissues and often in the blood.

lineman–a football player whose position is on the line of scrimmage.

remission–a state or period during which the symptoms of a disease are less intense.

senior–the final year of high school or college.

stunt–an unusual or daring action used to gain attention.

technology–the science of how something works.

tough–hard to destroy, hurt, or break.

tournament–a series of contests or games played to win a championship.

treatment–medical or surgical care for a sickness or an injury.

triple–having or involving three parts, things, or people.

ONLINE RESOURCES

Booklinks
NONFICTION NETWORK
FREE! ONLINE NONFICTION RESOURCES

To learn more about Roman Reigns, please visit **abdobooklinks.com** or scan this QR code. These links are routinely monitored and updated to provide the most current information available.

INDEX